FOLK SONGS

for Violin & Cello Duet

Arranged by Michelle Hynson

ISBN 978-1-70519-271-9

Visit Hal Leonard Online at
www.halleonard.com

World headquarters, contact:
Hal Leonard
7777 West Bluemound Road
Milwaukee, WI 53213
Email: info@halleonard.com

In Europe, contact:
Hal Leonard Europe Limited
1 Red Place
London, W1K 6PL
Email: info@halleonardeurope.com

In Australia, contact:
Hal Leonard Australia Pty. Ltd.
4 Lentara Court
Cheltenham, Victoria, 3192 Australia
Email: info@halleonard.com.au

Contents

ANIMAL FAIR

American Folksong

AULD LANG SYNE

Words by Robert Burns
Traditional Scottish Melody

THE BAND PLAYED ON

Words by John E. Palmer
Music by Charles B. Ward

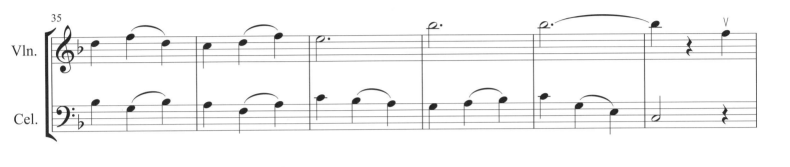

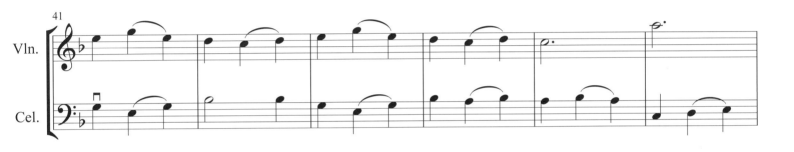

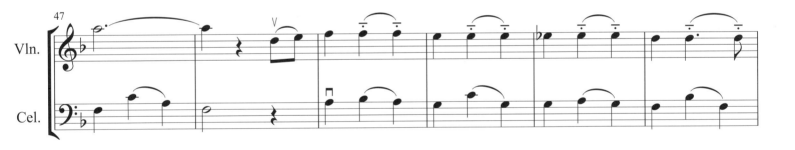

BEAUTIFUL DREAMER

Words and Music by
Stephen C. Foster

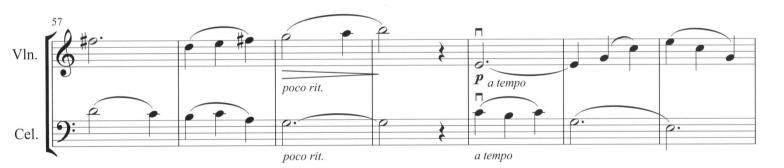

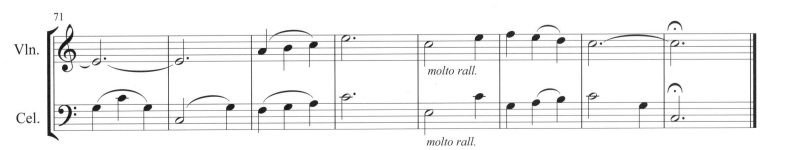

BLOW THE MAN DOWN

Traditional Sea Chantey

DANNY BOY

Words by Frederick Edward Weatherly
Traditional Irish Folk Melody

DOWN BY THE RIVERSIDE

African American Spiritual

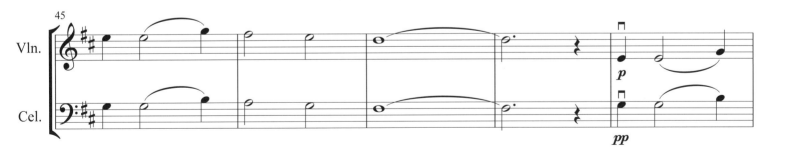

DRINK TO ME ONLY WITH THINE EYES

Lyrics by Ben Jonson
Traditional Music

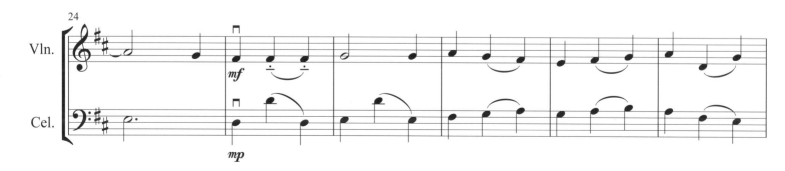

THE ERIE CANAL

Traditional New York Work Song

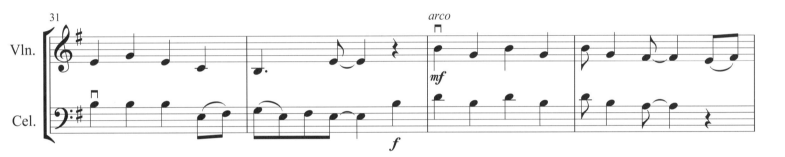

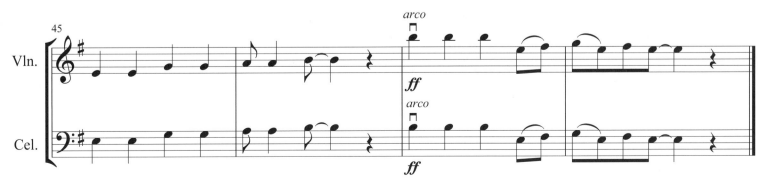

FOR HE'S A JOLLY GOOD FELLOW

Traditional

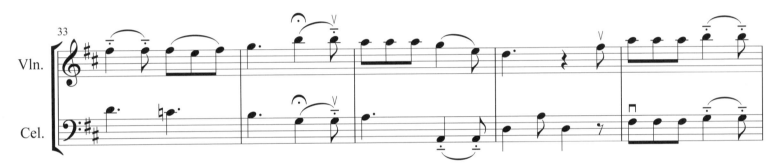

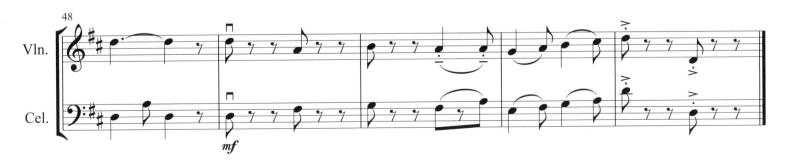

FRÉRE JACQUES MEETS THREE BLIND MICE

FRÉRE JACQUES (Are You Sleeping?)
Traditional

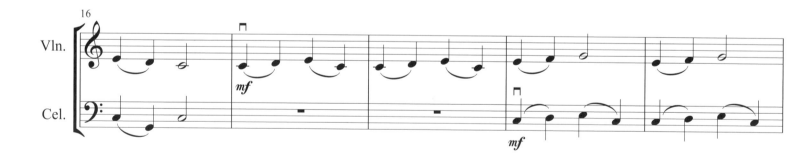

THREE BLIND MICE
Traditional

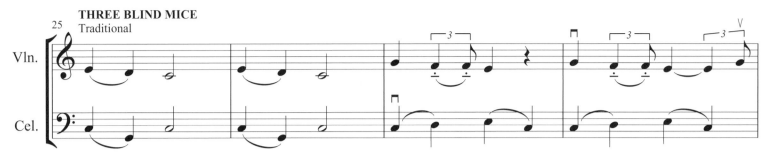

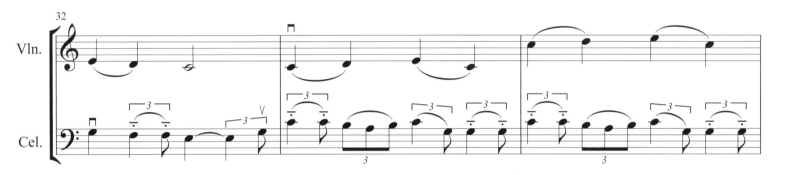

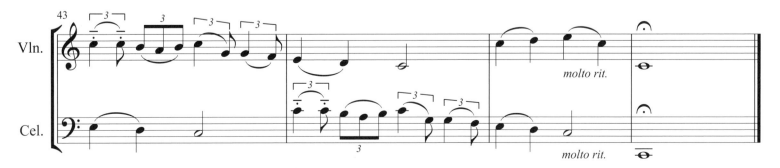

HE'S GOT THE WHOLE WORLD IN HIS HANDS

Traditional Spiritual

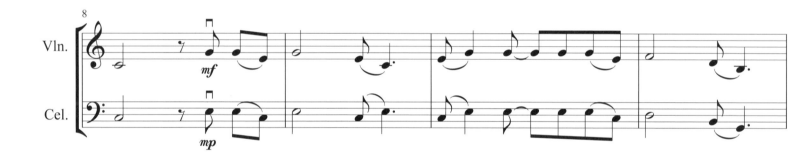

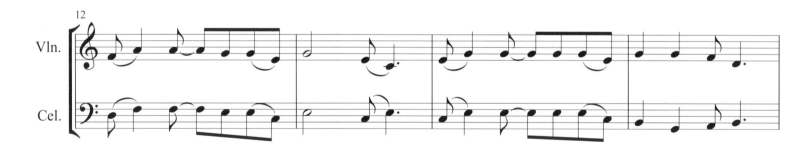

HOME ON THE RANGE

Lyrics by Dr. Brewster Higley
Music by Dan Kelly

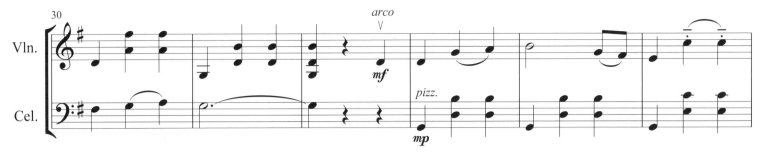

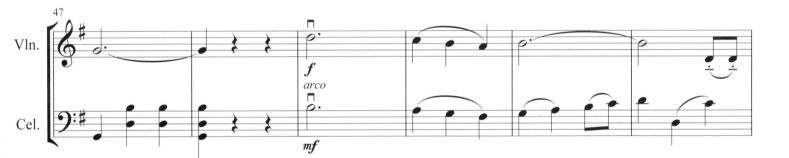

JEANIE WITH THE LIGHT BROWN HAIR

Words and Music by
Stephen C. Foster

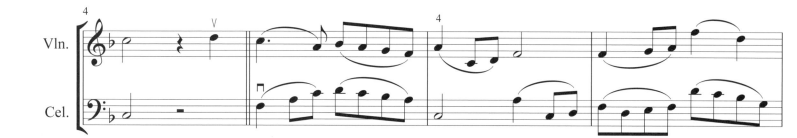

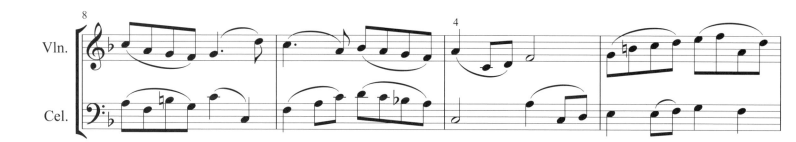

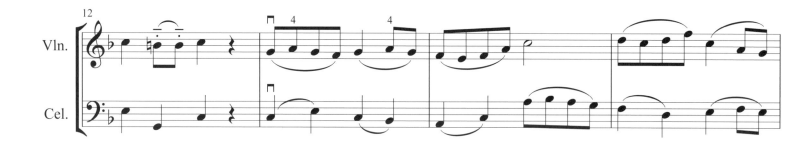

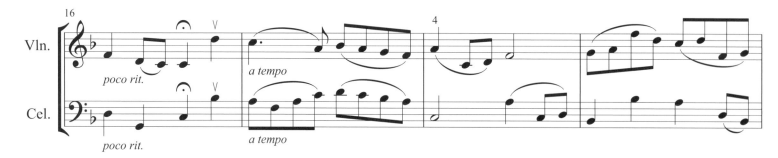

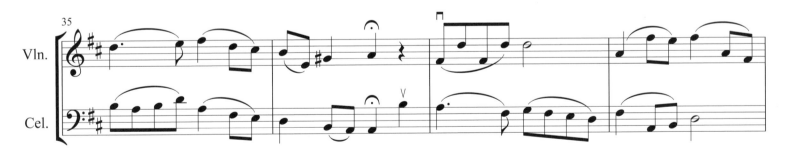

MY BONNIE LIES OVER THE OCEAN

Traditional

Like a Waltz

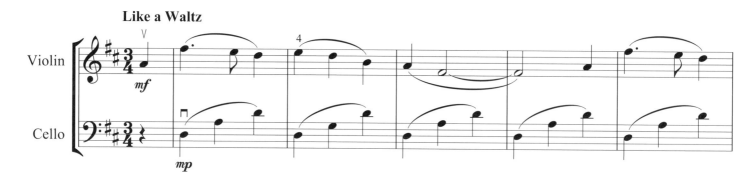

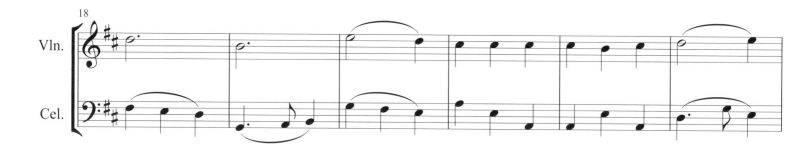

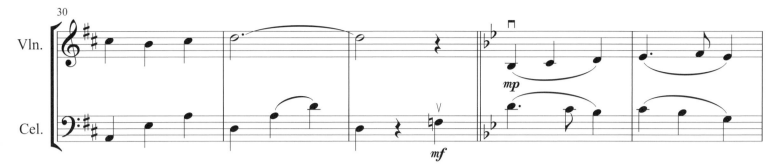

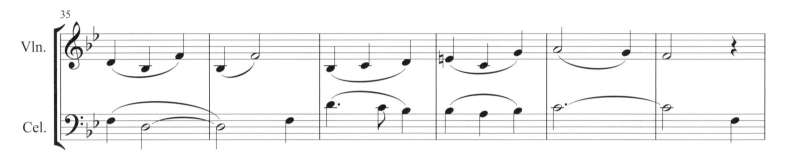

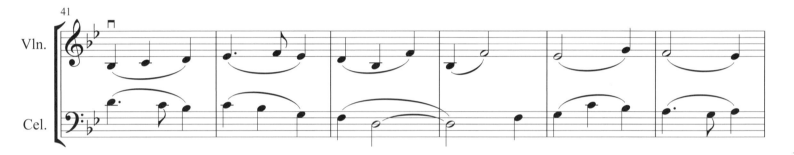

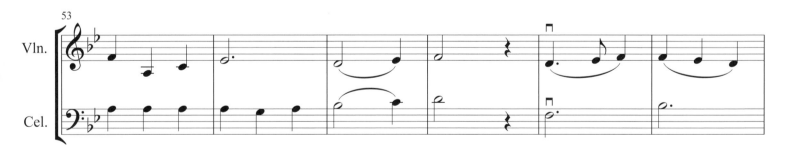

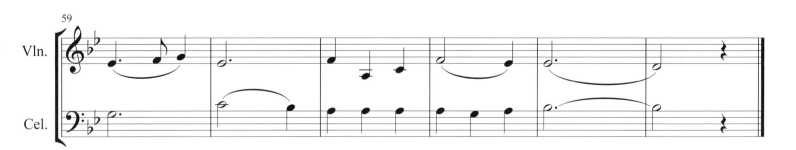

MY WILD IRISH ROSE

By Chauncey Olcott

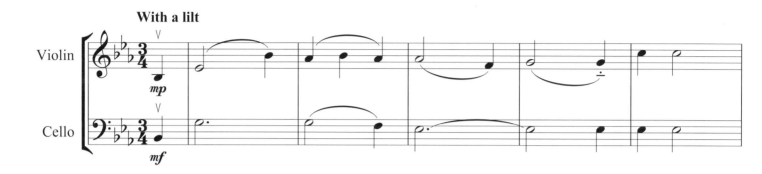

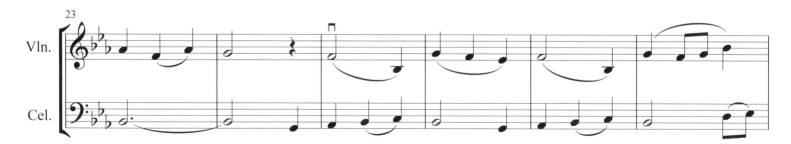

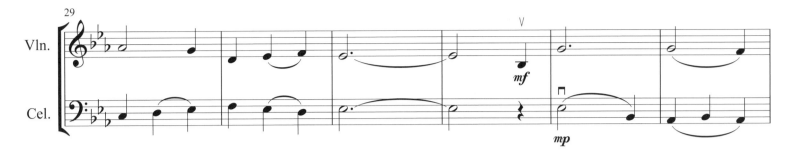

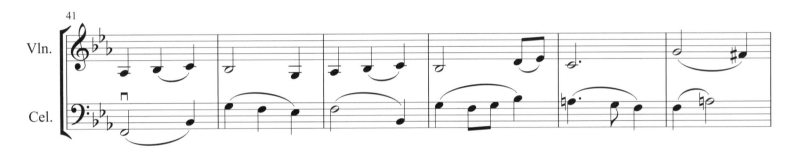

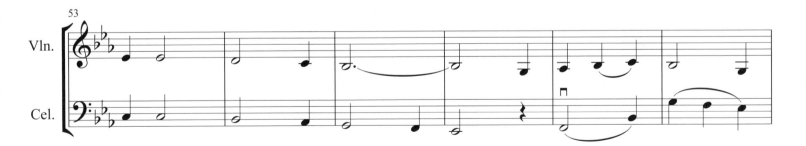

NOBODY KNOWS THE TROUBLE I'VE SEEN

African American Spiritual

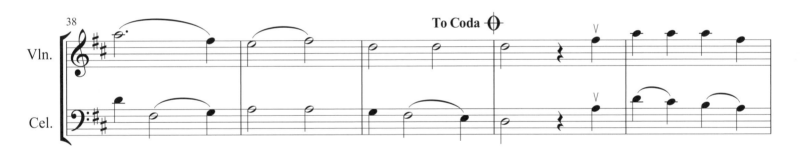

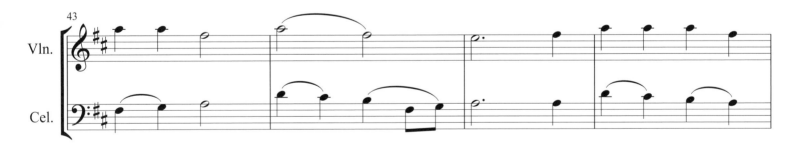

POP! GOES THE WEASEL

Traditional

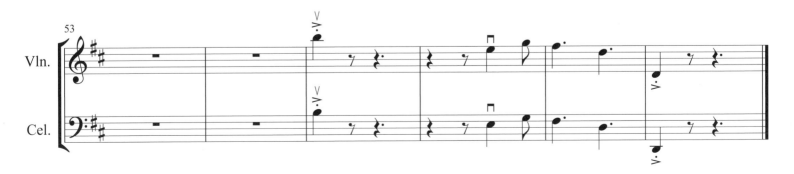

THE RED RIVER VALLEY

Traditional American Cowboy Song

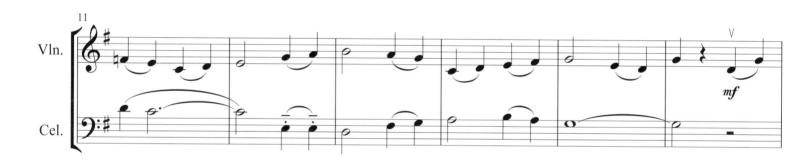

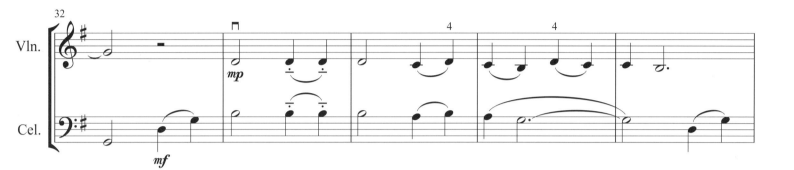

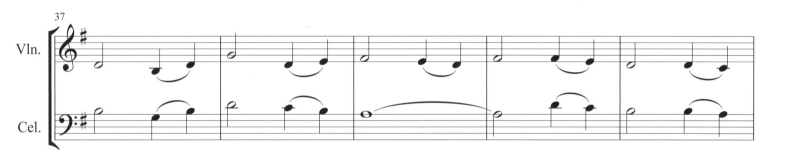

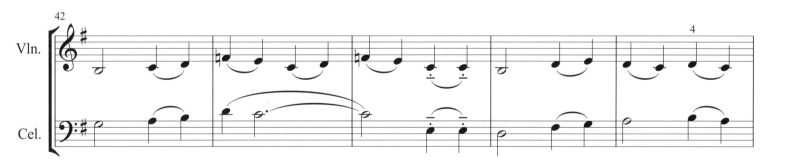

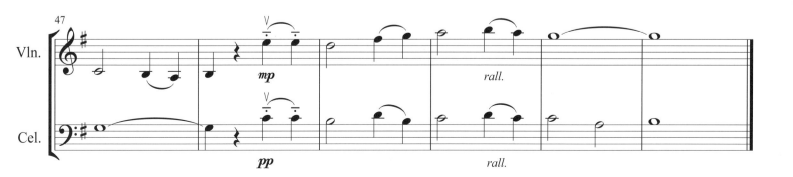

SANTA LUCIA

By Teodoro Cottrau

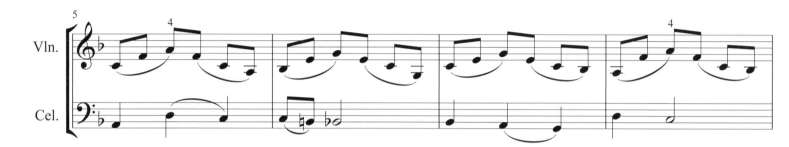

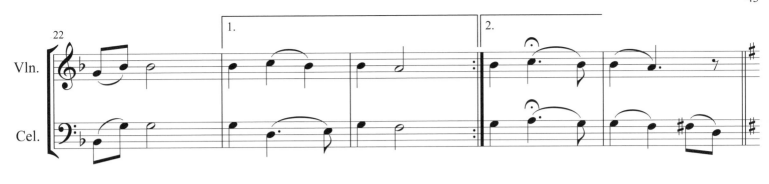

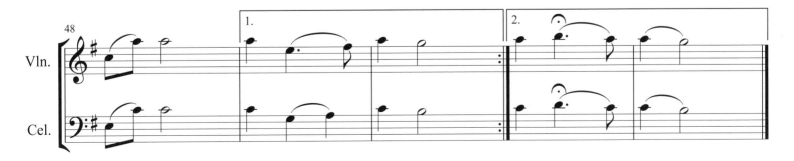

SCARBOROUGH FAIR

Traditional English

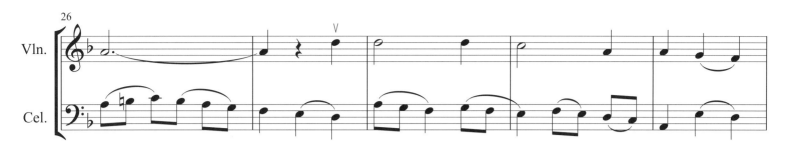

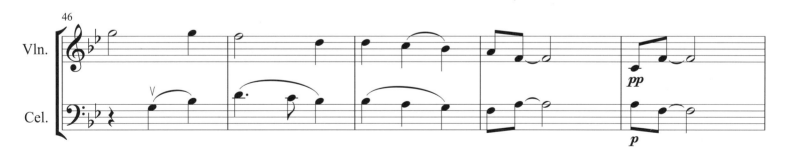

SHE'LL BE COMIN' 'ROUND THE MOUNTAIN

Traditional

SHENANDOAH

American Folksong

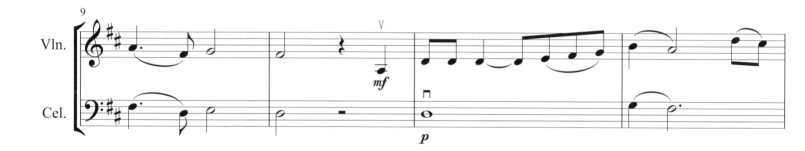

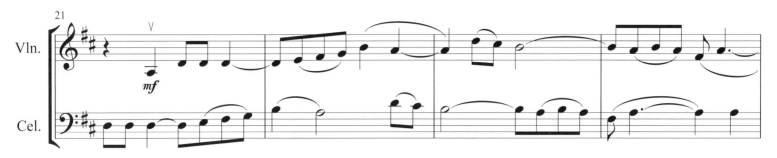

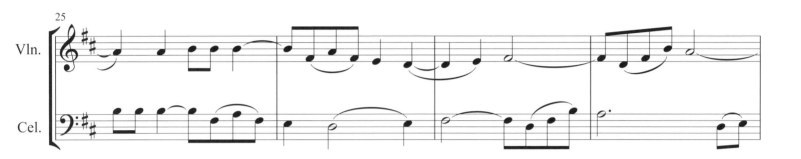

SIMPLE GIFTS

Traditional Shaker Hymn

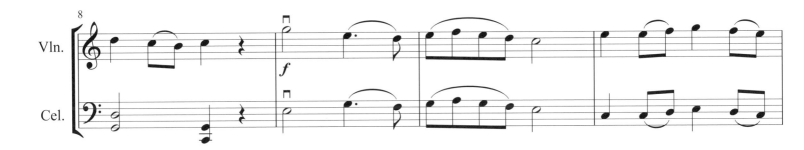

THE STREETS OF LAREDO

American Cowboy Song

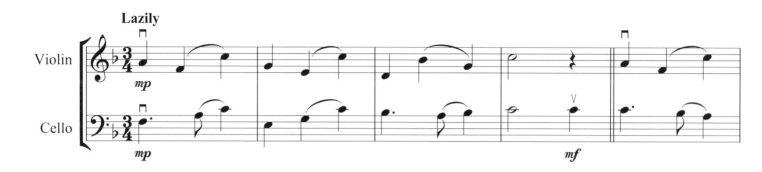

TAKE ME OUT TO THE BALL GAME

Words by Jack Norworth
Music by Albert von Tilzer

TURKEY IN THE STRAW

American Folksong

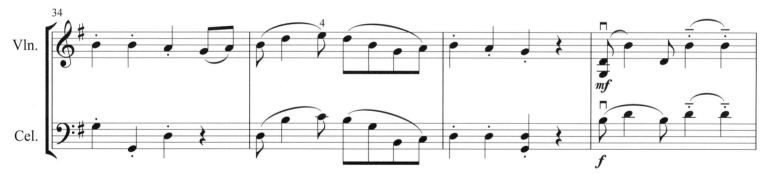

THE WABASH CANNON BALL

Hobo Song

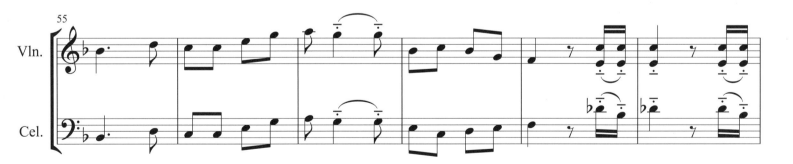

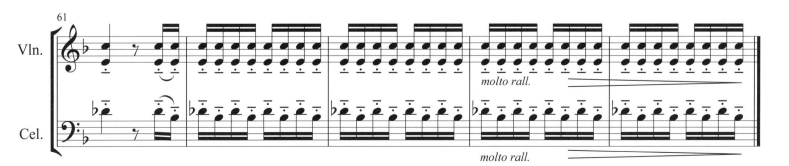

WHEN JOHNNY COMES MARCHING HOME

Words and Music by
Patrick Sarsfield Gilmore

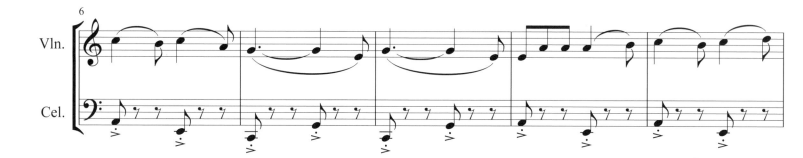

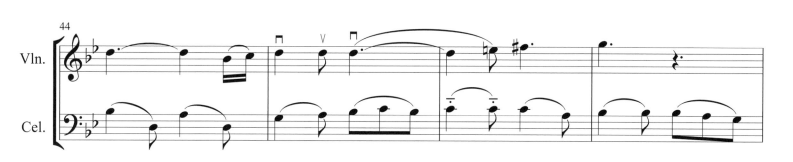

THE YELLOW ROSE OF TEXAS

Words and Music by
J.K., 1858

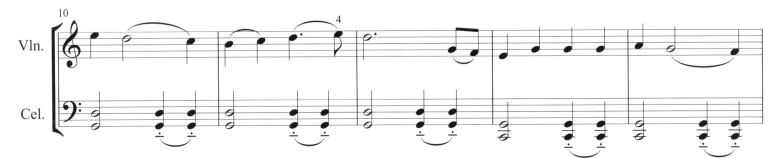

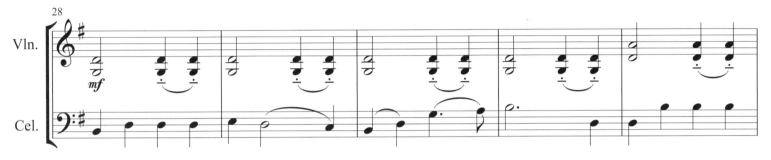

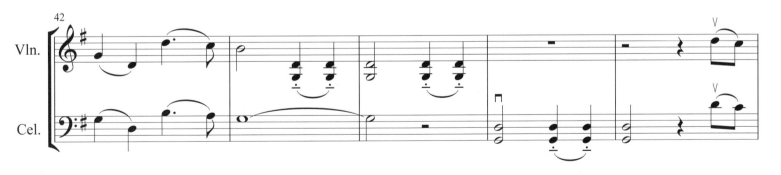

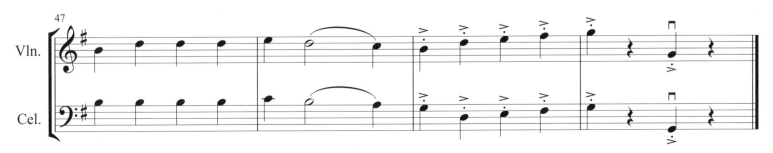

VIOLIN DUET
COLLECTIONS

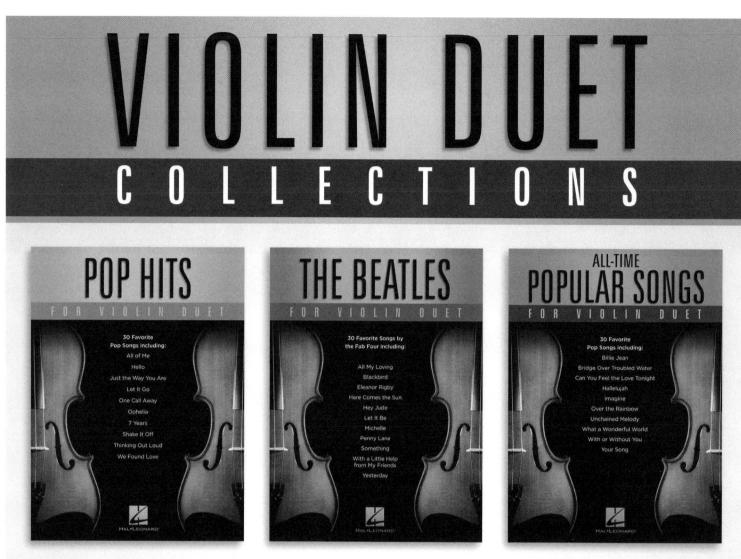

These collections are designed for violinists familiar with first position and comfortable reading basic rhythms. Each two-page arrangement includes a violin 1 and violin 2 part, with each taking a turn at playing the melody for a fun and challenging ensemble experience.

ALL-TIME POPULAR SONGS FOR VIOLIN DUET

Billie Jean • Bridge over Troubled Water • Can You Feel the Love Tonight • Hallelujah • Imagine • Over the Rainbow • Unchained Melody • What a Wonderful World • With or Without You • Your Song and more.

00222449 . . . . $14.99

THE BEATLES FOR VIOLIN DUET

All My Loving • Blackbird • Eleanor Rigby • A Hard Day's Night • Hey Jude • Let It Be • Michelle • Ob-La-Di, Ob-La-Da • Something • When I'm Sixty-Four • Yesterday and more.

00218245 . . . . $14.99

POP HITS FOR VIOLIN DUET

All of Me • Hello • Just the Way You Are • Let It Go • Love Yourself • Ophelia • Riptide • Say Something • Shake It Off • Story of My Life • Take Me to Church • Thinking Out Loud • Wake Me Up! and more.

00217577 . . . . $14.99

DISNEY SONGS FOR VIOLIN DUET

Beauty and the Beast • Can You Feel the Love Tonight • Colors of the Wind • Do You Want to Build a Snowman? • Hakuna Matata • How Far I'll Go • I'm Wishing • Let It Go • Some Day My Prince Will Come • A Spoonful of Sugar • Under the Sea • When She Loved Me • A Whole New World and more.

00217578 . . . . $14.99

HAL•LEONARD®
www.halleonard.com

Prices, contents, and availability subject to change without notice.